ACCLAIM ~~~

This book will help people manifest and realize their desires! I believe that putting the feelings with these positive affirmations can help people change their lives and accelerate their desired results in a shorter period of time. This book will deliver the magic to create all your desires if you honestly want to make a change in your life and empower yourself. Not only is Kimberly thoroughly educated in psychology, understands how the mind works and has great people skills, she also walks her talk and I am so honored to be her friend.

- Marianne Noad, Wholistic Health Practitioner/Diamond Producer

I believe that positive word statements are your GPS in life. Our minds take us to where we are going but our words bring our thoughts into manifestation. There is no way I would have become the person I am today nor attracted the success I have today without positive affirmations. This is not hogwash. Positive Affirmations WORK! Kimberly Phillips is right on point with the value and importance of positive words and affirmations. They're vital to one's health, wealth, and overall existence. She is someone who walks the walk and talks the talk. I appreciate her genuineness to serve others first before she serves herself. She is a tremendous leader and cares to lift up the lowest spirits of anyone she ever encounters. I've watched her in person speak words of life into others and witnessed the immediate transformation in that person's being. Kimberly Phillips is a Diamond of all Diamonds and truly a blessing to us all.

- **Emmanuel Bernstein**, Diamond Producer

Affirmations have played the biggest role in my success because I understand the power of words and how they create everything in our lives. Everything you want to accomplish in your life is 1 word away from you. I have been speaking affirmations for the last 7 years of my life. Consequently, everything I have drawn into my life, I actually spoke it into existence (e.g. mentors, finances, opportunities, etc). I believe that this book will give you a lot of choices as to what you can affirm to access your desired results. I also believe that if you apply the principles Kimberly is teaching you in this book, you may possibly be able to accomplish your desired results in a shorter period of time.

- **David Imonitie**, Million Dollar Producer

SAY IT UNTIL YOU SEIZE IT!

SAY IT UNTIL YOU SEIZE IT!

AFFIRMATIONS FOR NETWORKERS

WRITTEN BY:

KIM PHILLIPS

ISBN 13:978-1481084888
ISBN 10:1481084887

Printed in the United States of America

Cover Design by: E.S. Young

ACKNOWLEDGEMENTS

Every main actress has a supporting cast that deserves to be acknowledged.

Holton and Earlene Buggs: Thank you for countless hours and years of coaching and even intense mentoring in this industry and life. Thanks for setting such a great example for me to follow and teaching me the importance of affirming my goals. I totally respect your diligence and personal development to become the mentors you've become and the leadership principles you've taught me along the way that proved necessary to thrive in life and in this industry. I totally concur with most who regard you as the Michael Jordan of this industry. Thanks for being such incredible sponsors and friends.

Wanda Faye Briggs: How can I ever say thank you enough, not only to the one who gave me life, but to the "BEST MOM IN THE WHOLE-WIDE WORLD". You literally amaze me with your strength and encouragement. You are my unsung hero and definitely the wind beneath my wings. You literally carried me through this entire project and I am eternally grateful!

James Mitchell: You are the best dad a girl could ever have. Thanks for your encouragement and unwavering belief in me. Your love and emails with such heartfelt words of inspiration literally lifted me and helped me progress through this project. You are literally a perseverance specialist and I learned from the best.

Sharmane Miller: Thank you for always believing in me and encouraging me throughout the entire process and holding me accountable. Thanks for also helping me proof my work prior to submitting to copyeditors although you were seemingly overwhelmed with your doctorial research and assignments. Sometimes I wonder how did I attract such a wonderful sister and best friend like you into my life and sustain such a close friendship for over 20 years.

Rod Smith: Thank you for holding me accountable and literally provoking me to complete some of my unfinished projects that I kept talking about, namely this book. Not only have you been a good brother, you have been one of the best friends a girl could ever have and an exceptional mid-wife for this project. When I got stuck a couple of times and called, the answer and advice just seemed to easily flow from your lips. I am also most appreciative of the annoying emails and texts encouraging me to push and checking my progress and asking "where the heck is that book Kim." Before I knew it, you had your offspring, many on your team, to also harass me about completing this book and talk about their need for this book.

Tyron McDaniel: Thank you for also being my brother and coming in toward the end to help me carry this baby to term. You were so encouraging and your feedback was priceless as well as the questions you asked me to help me process better.

Uncle Mac Spencer: Thanks for being such

an amazingly giving uncle and offering to financially commit to seeing my dream come to fruition. I so appreciate you coming in at the conclusion of this project and fueling the delivery. It was like I was stuck in a ditch and you became that wrecker that pulled me out!

Kiarra Lastie: Thank you for being such an amazing sister and being more excited about this project than me. You are an incredible friend and the kind of sister that most girls wish they had. Thanks for also encouraging and believing in me.

Dr. Carolyn Miller: Thank you so much for being the big sister that you have been to me and paving the way for me in the area of psychology or counseling. Thanks for believing in me and respecting my work so much that you called several times to say push because I need your book today. You have no idea how much that encouraged me that someone of your caliber respects my gifts and talents. You are the best "god-sister" a girl could ever desire.

Apostle Brian Butler: Thank you for being such an amazing brother and for literally joining your prayers and faith with mine to see this project through to completion. Thank you for literally carrying a copy of my book cover around in your Bible and committing to pray daily for this book and those it will bless.

Scooter Young: You are an amazingly talented young entrepreneur and brilliant graphic designer. It's so fun working alongside you to give vision to what's in my head. Thanks for your tireless gifts of art and design.

Joan Murray: Thanks for your advice and direction towards the end of this project. In many respects, you were like a skillful mid-wife who unselfishly devoted your time and attention to helping me through my delivery process especially during the end when the contractions were the most intense and painful.

Pastor Joel Osteen: Thanks for being such an amazing pastor and role model.

Vivian Washington: Thanks for praying for me and being such a great "guardian mother".

Team Dominion: Thanks for valuing and respecting my leadership. I am incredibly blessed to have been chosen to lead such a wonderful yet purposeful team of people who have embraced my leadership and coaching. I pray God continues to exceed your highest expectations for your endeavors.

May I say, I am most appreciative to my Lord and Savior Jesus Christ and His Holy Spirit for being such an amazing conductor who orchestrated situations, circumstances, events, resources, information, ability, strength, and inspiration as well as funds for me and the good of this project that I hope and pray helps every one who gets their hands on it.

I salute every Networker no matter what field, company or entity throughwhich you network. This book was written with you in mind; yet as you can see by the table of contents, it can be an asset to anyone who is committed to changing and improving their lives or laying hold of their dreams and desires.

TABLE OF CONTENTS

Introduction.............................*I*

1. Do Affirmations Really Work?...............1
2. Abundance...............................15
3. Acceptance/Self Acceptance...............19
4. Attracting & Servicing Customers........21
5. Belief..................................23
6. Billionaire Status......................27
7. Closing to Action.......................29
8. Confidence..............................31
9. Contacting & Inviting...................33
10. Creating & Maintaining Momentum......35
11. Decision Making.........................37
12. Diamond Status..........................39
13. Duplicating Masterfully................43
14. Following up Successfully...............47
15. Goal Attainment.........................49
16. I Am 51
17. Leadership..............................53
18. List Building...........................55
19. Massive Action..........................57
20. Mastering 3-Ways & Edification...........61

21. Millionaire Status................................65

22. Overcoming Fear of Failure..................67

23. Overcoming Fear of Success................71

24. Overcoming Frustration......................75

25. Overcoming Procrastination................79

26. People Magnet....................................81

27. People Skills.......................................83

28. Perseverance......................................87

29. Pin Achievement................................89

30. Promoting Effectively for Events...........91

31. Public Speaking/Communicating.........95

32. Retention..97

33. Self-Discipline...................................99

34. Successful...101

35. Teamwork/Team Development..........103

36. Time & Life Management...................105

37. Work Ethic.......................................107

38. Say It Unitl You Seize It Self-Contract 109

INTRODUCTION

WHAT ARE AFFIRMATIONS?

Affirmations are statements or self-scripts you repeat to yourself until they become beliefs that are deposited into your subconscious mind which then passes the baton onto your actions to attract your desired results. Consider affirmations as a team of words synergistically working together to accomplish a significant yet common goal. What is the goal? I'm glad you asked! The goal is to effectively deliver an important message or proclamation to the part of your mind (subconscious/unconscious mind) that influences your actions (behavior) and consequently attracts your results.

GOAL: PERMEATE SUBCONSCIOUS MIND

I had the following visual as I studied to teach my team about the subconscious mind and how to properly influence it to get their desired results. Imagine with me, if you will, that there is an audience inside of your mind (let's refer to it as your "mental audience") and you are the speaker. Your goal is to deliver a message to your audience in the language they can understand and inspire them to take action. After much research and deliberation, you realize that this particular audience really gets fired up about carrying out instructions when the message is given with much fervor and intense emotions. More specifically, you also need to keep in mind that there is a strong correlation or relationship between the type of emotion exhibited during the speech and your audience's results. For ex ample, when you emit positive emotions as you deliver your message, your "mental audience" carries out positive actions and attracts positively desired results. However, when you emit negative emotions, your inner audience carries out negative actions and brings back negative results. In addition to delivering an emotionally stimulating message to your mental audience, it is also very important to create a picture in the mind of your audience as you instruct, inspire, and invigorate them. I certainly pray that the affirmations in this book assist you to do just that. Kim Phillips has a psychology background and has been thoroughly educated (formally as well as personally) on how the mind works. Her goal is to educate, enlighten, and empower you to get your desired results using the affirmations in this book along with the wisdom intricately interwoven in their fabric.

The visual of a "mental audience" was provided for those of you who have a negative script flashing on the screen of your mental canvas as you affirm your results or find it challenging to embrace the philosophy of "self-talk". Perhaps, you may have a better encounter with your affirmations if you embrace the idea that you are communicating to an audience who resides in your subconscious (unconscious) mind. (**Side note:** *I apologize to any of my psychology colleagues who find it challenging to embrace the term "subconscious mind". I recommend you translate it into the formal terms we learned in school as opposed to "throwing the baby away with the bath water"*).

Although this book was written with the networker in mind, it is certainly inclusive of almost anyone who is committed to influencing and reprogramming their mind to manifest their desired results.

THE MAIN INGREDIENTS

The 3 main ingredients needed to help you manifest your desired results are:

- Words
- Images
- Emotions (W.I.E).

This book provides you the words that will help you paint the appropriate image on your mental canvas; however, you must provide the emotions and pre-play what you desire to experience prior to manifesting it. It is also helpful to remember that the main agent you are influencing is your subconscious mind and it doesn't really know the difference between what is "real" or "imagined".

WHY DID I WRITE THIS BOOK?

For the inquiring minds who desire to know, I wrote this book simply because I saw a need and felt equipped and commissioned to meet it. I have been a student of affirmations and self-talk long before I received any formal or personal education regarding them. I simply bought into the philosophy that "death and life are in the power of the tongue". I am also a strong believer that everything in the natural was spoken into existence by voice-activating words with intense belief and emotions.

I am a network marketing industry ambassador and am blessed to have been a full-time net-working professional in excess of eight years. Prior to engaging this industry, I thoroughly enjoyed helping people as a social worker and providing preliminary counseling. As a leader is often taught, when you see a pur-poseful need that you can satisfy, meet it.

During the times I was afforded an opportunity to lead, train, and interact with others in the industry, I realized the words many of my col-leagues used were incongruent with their de-sired results, yet they believed in the power of words. I noticed that I was constantly correct-ing and instructing them on a better way to ex-press them without negatively impacting their results. Before I knew it, several people began asking me to look over their affirmations and correct them. Moreover, there were countless others who requested that I write them a per-sonal affirmation to help them achieve their goals. Shortly thereafter, many began referring to me as "the affirmation queen". This book has the capacity to bring out the winner in you. If you are reading this book, I strongly believe you are a winner and it is your time to win!

CHAPTER 1
DO AFFIRMATIONS REALLY WORK?

This is a very prevalent question. Many people curiously ask if affirmations really work; however, I personally believe this is not the best question to ask in this situation. It is very important to choose our questions wisely because the answers we get in life are in direct proportion to the questions we ask. The question we should ask here is how can I make my affirmations work better for me? Or what can I do to increase my effectiveness with my affirmations?

My answer: Most definitely, affirmations work for those who work them effectively. In fact, 15 components or helpful pointers have been developed to help **YOU** work the affirmations instead of you waiting on them to magically work for you. All of the components start with the letter "P" and are written in an alliterative form to make it easier for you to remember.

15 STEPS TO AFFIRMATION SUCCESS: FOR BEST RESULTS

1. PERSONAL:

The most effective affirmations are personal. Use "I" statements as often as possible. Make the affirmation inclusive of you (I, Me, and My).

- Effective: I thoroughly enjoy living the #1 lifestyle in the world.

- Ineffective: The #1 lifestyle in the world is enjoyable. (For who? – how about for you).

In the above example of the "ineffective" statement, this affirmation does not indicate that you are the one living the #1 lifestyle in the world. Making the affirmation general like this may result in you becoming aware of others around you living this #1 lifestyle but not you. Moreover, you stating the affirmation this way also sends a message that you are actually excluding yourself from this experience since you excluded yourself in the statement. For best results, connect the goal to you by making your affirmation personal.

2. PRESENT TENSED:

Your affirmation should be "now-focused." Imagine that what you desire already exists but in an unseen arena (future) and your word statements are designed to transfer what is in your future over into your present situation. To manifest what you desire in the future, you have to say, see and feel it as if it is presently happening.

Using the word "will" is a future-tensed word and indicates something is expected at a later time in the future. In fact, the word "will" keeps your desired results in the future which never catches up with your present. So your results, in this instance, also seem afar off. Remember your goal is to get it to happen now!

• Effective: I AM so happy and grateful NOW that I am a diamond consultant in xyz company by Xyz date.

• Ineffective: I will be a diamond consultant in

Xyz Company.

- Effective: This IS a good year for me!

- Ineffective: This is GOING TO BE a good year for me.

3. POSITIVE:

Your affirmation should be stated positively with the goal of playing the game to win as opposed to not losing. Your focus here should be what you desire to happen and not what you don't want to happen. Do everything in your power to stay away from words that even indicate lack or loss. The words "want, never, won't, will not" and "without," indicate a deficiency.

If the emotion you feel or the picture you see in your mind's eye elicit a negative emotion for you, you might want to examine your affirmation and rearrange your words with a goal of producing a positive emotion and a peaceful "inside-environment" or mental attitude.

- Effective: My team and I accomplish our desired goals by the middle of the month.

- Ineffective: My team and I do not wait until the end of the month to accomplish our goals.

- Effective: I am timely and love being on time for all of my appointments.

- Ineffective: I am never late for my appointments.

3

4. PRECISE:

Be as specific as possible and descriptively articulate your desired results so that it crystallizes the picture on your mental canvas. Many people use vague statements like "I am financially-free". What does that look like? Describe it so it paints a more vivid picture for you. Remember we think in pictures. Your subconscious mind is looking for the file that has pictures of financial freedom.

- Effective: I earn $10,000 a month!

- Ineffective: I make a lot of money

- Effective: I retire from Xyz company on or before xyz date.

- Ineffective: I retire early (When?)

5. PASSIONATELY-EMOTED:

"Emotionalizing" your affirmations will help you speedily manifest your desired results. I recommend you say your affirmation with feeling and use words that elicit positive emotions. Make it a goal to use "emotive-based" words to stimulate the type of emotional excitement, joy and gratitude that you anticipate experiencing once you manifest your desired results in the natural. In other words, don't wait till the battle is over; SHOUT NOW! Ask yourself, "Now how would I feel when I achieve my goal?" Begin to feel that way now as you state your affirmation.

Experience the emotion now!

- Effective: It feels so good to make 6 figures on a monthly basis.

- Ineffective: I want to make 6 figures on a monthly basis.

6. PICTURED VIVIDLY:

You materialize what you visualize! In life we tend to get what we picture because we actually think in pictures. Remember, if you can see it, then you can seize it! I recommend you daily make time to close your eyes and meditate on your desired results while in a relaxed state. Initially, it may be helpful to focus on your breathing because it helps you erase all thoughts from your mental canvas and start with a blank slate. Breathe normal! Now you are ready to create a picture of the image you desire on the canvas of your imagination. Make sure you include yourself in the image and crystallize the image by using your emotions (feel the way you would feel as mentioned in the above section. If your picture is blurry, which may initially be the case, keep crystallizing your picture until it comes into clear focus. You will accelerate toward your desired goals when you have clarity of vision.

I recommend you do what I call "success-proofing" your surroundings by posting pictures of what you desire. For instance, if you desire a certain car, then go get a brochure or take a picture of yourself with the car when you go to test drive it. As Napoleon Hill recommends, write your goal on index cards and keep one with you in the car. Use a different card for each goal and don't focus on more than 5 affirmations at a time.

7. PURPOSEFUL:

I strongly recommend you take time out to write down what you really desire to accomplish. Successful people make it a practice to begin with the end in mind and establish a chief aim or definite or specific desire. You will be surprised how many people have no idea or have never given deep thought to what it is they actually desire in life. Many think they have no say in their outcomes and must just play with the hand they were dealt. Then there is a large number of people who conform to what society or credible others in their lives tell them their goals should be. Consequently, these individuals find themselves struggling to reach a goal that they think may grant them the acceptance they long for, yet still it leaves them unfulfilled and possibly frustrated because it contradicts their root desire.

8. PRINCIPLE-BASED VERSUS PRESUMPTION:

Make sure your affirmation is not geared to challenge universal laws (e.g. the law of sowing and reaping, law of gravity, law of polarity, law of attraction or vibration, etc.). Please keep in mind that affirmations are not geared to control others. It also helps if you affirm "realistically possible goals" and gradually increase them. For example, If you have never made $3,000 a month, you might easily affirm and manifest $10,000 monthly income prior to affirming

$150,000 a month.

9. PREDICATED UPON BELIEF AND SELF-IMAGE:

How do you see yourself? You are designed to function in concert with your self-portrait or how you see yourself. It is widely believed that we talk to ourselves a lot more often than we realize. Several have noticed an inner battle going on between their "inside-voice" and "outside-voice" as they repeat their affirmations aloud. For instance, you affirm, "I am wealthy". Then your inner voice says, "You're lying, you are broke as a joke and can't pay attention." (This is a negative script that must be replaced). Some research will recommend that you start out gradually by altering the affirmation to say something like, "I deserve to be wealthy" or "I am becoming wealthy." The word 'becoming' slyly gets your affirmation a hall pass to travel on to your subconscious mind until you do more repair on your positive self-belief.

10. PROFESSED OR PENNED REPEATEDLY:

Repetition is definitely the mother of all skills as it has been known to incubate, give birth to and nurse the skills we develop over a course of time. It is recommended that you commit to either profess (say) or pen (write) your affirmations daily until you achieve your desired results. For best results, commit to saying or writing your affirmations in the morning when you awake and right before you go to sleep. This is the time that your mind is the most pliable. Imagine you are a farmer and you desire to plant choice seeds (words) in your soil (mind). Many farmers will tell you that there is a time to sow or plant and a time to reap (harvest). In this instance, the best time for you to plant the seed of your affirmation in the soil of your mind is when your mind is most conducive to receiving the seed (so to speak).

11. PERSISTENTLY PERFORMED:

For best results, resolve that you desire your goals so much that you are willing to commit to daily repeating your affirmations and bringing your actions into alignment with what you seek. You may find it helpful to also design and focus on how you plan to reward yourself when you achieve your desired results. For example, I positively motivated myself to achieve a desired pin promotion by making an agreement with myself that once I achieved my goal, I would reward myself by moving to a particular high-rise luxury condominium and purchasing my dream bedroom set. Prior to achieving the goal, I selected my reward and daily escaped my current situation every night before bed to visit this bed and luxury place online while building my business in a foreign country. This practice helped me persevere by shifting my focus from any discomfort or intense work ethic to the reward. I still remember being in awe when I manifested my results and subsequently my dream bedroom set and place of residence.

12. PATIENTLY ANTICIPATED:

I would be remiss in my responsibility if I didn't warn you that it is highly unlikely that your situation will change overnight. Affirmations are not a quick fix to all your challenges. Be persistent and give yourself time to manifest your desired results. In many cases, it has taken you years to program yourself to think the way you think and it may take time for you to replace negative scripts with positive ones. In this industry, we are often taught the importance of managing the expectations of those we lead. Since I am leading you through this subject matter regarding effective affirmations, I am taking the liberty to encourage you to manage your expectations. By the way, don't be surprised if you encounter opposition or tests prior to receiving your promise or promotion. It's just part of the process. In school, tests always precede promotions. Just remember you are equipped, and this is just a test to see "how badly you want it."

If you are willing to wait forever, it is very unlikely that you will have to wait that long. I understand that life is filled with a plethora of opportunities to develop patience, and you may feel like you have been in a waiting room almost all of your life. You have to wait to be born. You have to wait to die. Many times there are testing opportunities (adversities) that interestingly enhance your wait time and challenge your commitment to stay the course. If you understand that it is just part of the process to achieving your desired results, you will pass the test with flying colors and enjoy your promotion. Trials, tribulations, and adversities are all designed to help solidify the promotion you seek. Waiting is part of the process; however, how you wait is extremely significant. I want to encourage you to do whatever is necessary to keep a good "inside-environment" as you wait. Also make sure you walk in forgiveness and peace with everyone so it doesn't hinder the manifestation of your desired outcome.

13. PRAISE INDUCED:

We bring about what we thank about! Remember it is better to work from a place of victory and not defeat. In my opinion, having an attitude of gratitude is very instrumental in helping you keep a good "inside-environment" and maintaining a grateful heart. This is very important because it helps you work congruent with the law of vibration or attraction which has as its premise that "we bring about what we think and thank about" and "what we focus on expands and gravitates toward us".

I recommend that you do a self-assessment of your assets and strengths and express gratitude for them (what exists already in the natural as well as what you desire to manifest soon). Most of the times we focus on what we need to change as opposed to what is already going well for us. Giving praise helps redirect your focus and mood which are both very important in helping you manifest your desired results. Many strategists recommend you even enhance your affirmation by starting off saying, "I am so happy and grateful now that _____(you fill in the blank) as mentioned on "The Secret" documentary film. Have fun and intentionally emote positive emotions as you give thanks!

14. PREPARED "PRE-PLAYS":

I bet you never thought that having imaginary friends and playing "make-believe" as a child would really come in handy one day. I totally recommend you sit down and think through how you can "pre-play" and prepare for the results you are expecting to manifest. Let's say you desire to be promoted to a certain advancement level in your company. Well, you should pay attention to and model others who are already doing what you desire to do. Have a dress rehearsal. When you attend events, dress so sharp that others think you are the speaker or leader. Go on the stage when no one is around and pretend to give your story once you "earn the right to be heard" on that particular platform.

If they play theme music, pick yours out ahead of time and play it often, closing your eyes as you visualize and role play your desired experience. If the people in your company go through an award ceremony, get your leader to act as if you are being awarded and have someone else video it or take a picture of the experience so you can refer back to it later. One of the key components is that you think and feel the way you would like to think and feel when you really qualify for the award or experience.

15. PARTNERSHIP SUPPORTED:

I totally love having accountability partners! I noticed that I follow through with my commitments when I know I am expected to give an account to someone. Be selective as to who you choose as an accountability partner. For best results, choose someone who is positively sup portive and has a vested interest in your success (a spouse, close family member, coach, mentor, mastermind group, or success-buddy).

Find out from your accountability partner what is the best way for you to inform them that you completed your task at hand (e.g. phone call, text, email, etc..) My best friend, Sharmane, and I have literally helped one another through every degree program effectively using this method, and currently we are both pursuing our doctorate degrees as we build our network marketing businesses. We share with one another our desired volume or how many papers we have to write, along with the deadline date, and how often we plan to check in with the other until it is completed. Along the way, we tend to celebrate the other for performing the activity or accomplishing our desired goal. This really comes in handy during the times I'm challenged to stay the course.

It is also important that you select someone who will not be too soft and let you off the hook. During the course of writing this book, one of my success partners, Rod, who happens to be one of my best friends, sent me an email saying, "Kim, where in the heck is that book. I need it!" I laughed but it really put fire under me to complete my assignment. Remember, it is not wise to share your goals with everyone as some people are inconspicuous "dream-killers" and "dream-stealers".

CHAPTER 2
ABUNDANCE

I am abundantly supplied.

All of my needs are met with the best.

I have plenty more to put in store.

I always have enough for me and enough to share.

I am a "money-magnet."

Money and profitable ideas flow to me with ease and without much effort.

I am a check magnet and check collector.

I save, sow, and invest the right amount of money.

I always receive the greatest return on my investment of time, effort, money and service.

My talents and abilities attract wealth.

I am spiritually, financially, and emotionally wealthy.

I attract wealth on a daily basis.

I know about, recognize, and respond to great and profitable opportunities.

People love to sow large amounts of money and profitable ideas into my life.

I capitalize on ideas, concepts, and inventions that increase my profit potential.

I have very healthy bank accounts and my money is safe with various lending institutions.

I am wise in my investments and seek wise counsel when necessary.

I prosper at all I set my hands to do.

My financial achievement and success is unlimited.

I prosper in my thinking.

I am a great money manager.

I am aware of and positively tap into the abundance that is all around me.

People who need or respect what I have to offer are attracted to me and possess the ability and desire to invest.

The more I serve others, the more I increase in abundance.

I accept abundance in my life.

I am so happy and grateful to have multiple sources of income flowing to me in abundance.

Dramatic wealth is a virtue I possess!

CHAPTER 3
ACCEPTANCE/SELF-ACCEPTANCE

I accept and approve of myself regardless of what others say or do.

I love myself.

I am self-assured.

I like being with myself.

I enjoy my own company.

I am great at being myself even when I am in the company of others.

I find myself interesting and absolutely amazing.

I validate myself and my own self-worth.

I am valuable.

I am one of the most amazing people I know.

I totally love my personality and it serves me well.

I am fully equipped to fulfill my purpose and life mission.

I enjoy being me.

It is so fun being me.

I am such a winner and all I do is win.

I respect and believe in myself.

I trust myself and my decisions.

I succeed at all I do!

I am super successful and I feel good about it.

I enjoy serving others and being served.

I am a tremendous giver and receiver.

I am good enough!

I am always worthy of love and acceptance.

CHAPTER 4
ATTRACTING & SERVICING CUSTOMERS

I am great at establishing rapport with people.

I am pleasant and in tune to the desires and needs of my customers.

I am great at attracting loyal retail and wholesale customers.

I am great at selling myself to my customers and they love being serviced by me.

My customers willingly refer others who desire what I have to offer.

I am great at exuding confidence and smiling as I make contact with my customers and potential customers.

I am great at engaging others in conversations about themselves and I actively listen to what they have to say.

I am great at repeating pertinent information my customers previously revealed to me showing great interest in them.

I always use words to which my customers can relate.

I am great at making my customers feel valued and important.

I am great at following through and delivering

on my promises to my customers.

I service _____ customers per month.

I acquire _____ new customers per month.

I am very knowledgeable about the product/services that I offer.

I believe in my product and service so much that I use and experience tremendous benefits from it.

I am great at asking the right questions and stimulating the right amount of interest from my potential customers.

I am great at showing appreciation to my customers.

I always have more than enough inventory to abundantly supply my customers.

I am unique, attractive, confident and utilize excellent customer service skills.

I am so happy and thankful that I have an excellent retention rate among my retail and wholesale customers.

CHAPTER 5
BELIEF

I only say and do things that support what I believe.

I am a product of what I believe and promote.

I vividly picture the success I desire.

All of my efforts and activities are congruent with what I believe.

I believe in myself and what I have to offer 100% of the time.

I surround myself with people and experiences that assist me with expanding my capacity to positively believe.

My belief in myself and what I promote is contagious and easily adopted by those I lead.

I am great at communicating what I believe.

I totally believe in my opportunity, product/service, leadership, and company, and it shows.

I think bigger and believe better than ever; therefore I receive the best results possible in all that I do.

I believe big; therefore, I receive big.

I am not moved by what I see, hear, or feel, only by what I believe.

I believe I prosper in all that I set my hands to

do.

I believe my results stand out among the rest because of my ability to believe bigger than others.

I am great at starving doubts while feeding my belief.

My actions and results are aligned with my belief that I win in all that I do.

I attract others who believe big.

All that I desire to achieve is possible because I believe.

All my beliefs are in harmony with my goals and purpose.

I easily release disempowering beliefs and I replace them with beliefs that serve me and my goals.

I allow myself to be positively influenced by empowering thoughts and beliefs.

I only surround myself with people, places, and things that reinforce my belief.

I easily redefine my life by redefining my beliefs.

I make room for what I expect to manifest in my life.

My subconscious and "reticular-activation-sys

tem" are positively programmed to bring about what I believe.

I expect and prepare for what I am believing to show up in my life.

I believe I can, therefore I do.

CHAPTER 6
BILLIONAIRE STATUS

I AM A BILLIONAIRE.

It feels so good to be a billionaire.

I talk like a billionaire.

I walk like a billionaire.

I live and give like a billionaire.

I love interacting with others who inspire my commitment to manifest and maintain billionaire status.

It feels so good to think bigger and better than I have ever thought before.

I love how my story inspires others to achieve billionaire status.

I love thinking multi-dimensional.

I attract the best minds and display value for my mastermind alliances.

Everything I touch prospers and multiplies.

All of my investments yield me the greatest returns.

I wisely invest my time, talents, and treasures in the most profitable people, opportunities, deals, events, ministries, charities, and enviroments.

I love inspiring and developing others into millionaire and billionaire status.

I am a great billionaire coach and I am committed to showing others how to create and sustain wealth.

I am a student of wealth and I am great at learning and applying wealth principles.

I am so happy and grateful to be a billionaire and possess great humility regardless of my status.

I understand the purpose for my billionaire status and properly use my influence and position as a billionaire to help uplift and inspire others.

I am an excellent giver and receiver.

I am so happy and grateful to be a billionaire and remain humble.

I have a billionaire mindset.

CHAPTER 7
CLOSING TO ACTION

I am great at presenting information in such a way that people who view my opportunity desire to get started right away with the top packages.

Everyone I expose to my opportunity either becomes a customer or business partner within 48 hours of exposure.

I am great at establishing rapport with my prospects.

I listen well to the needs of my prospects and make a great connection between their need and our opportunity.

I am great at finding solutions to my prospects' needs as it relates to this opportunity.

My excitement and belief about this opportunity is so positive and electrifying that others are looking forward to joining my organization.

I masterfully communicate the value for prospects to take advantage of timing and positioning with my company.

I am great at identifying my prospects' needs and finding solutions in line with what we have to offer.

I am great at creating and demonstrating a sense of urgency for what my company has to offer.

I am great at anticipating and handling potential objections.

During my presentation, I smoothly address common concerns, questions, and objections that relate to most prospects.

I am great at retrieving information for a prospective business partner and I easily walk them through how to initiate or engage the opportunity without them feeling forced.

People willingly release pertinent information to initiate their business after evaluating my opportunity.

I am great at discerning and listening to what the prospect deems as important to him or her and expounding only on issues relevant to their desires and needs.

I am great at demonstrating to my prospects that I am interested in them and what's important to them.

Upon making a positive buying decision, my prospects embrace the wisdom to immediately schedule a series of exposure opportunities.

It feels wonderful to have a _____ % "closing to action ratio".

CHAPTER 8
CONFIDENCE

I display unwavering confidence.

I am bold and courageous.

I radiate self-assuredness in all that I say and do.

Everything I touch prospers.

I excel at all I set my hands to do.

I am creative.

I am talented.

I am skilled and confident in my abilities.

I easily establish rapport with people.

I positively influence others.

Every time I speak, I electrify my audience.

I am a winner.

I am empowered and I am fully equipped to empower others.

I carry myself with the utmost respect and confidence.

Every day, I increase my confidence and belief in myself.

My behavior and demeanor show that I am

confident that winning is my only option.

I am a winner and all I do is win no matter what.

I am unstoppable.

I believe in myself 100% of the time.

I have endless possibilities.

I love myself for who I am.

I deserve to win and succeed in business and in life.

I am attractive.

I look extremely successful.

I associate with and attract other successful people to my life.

I trust myself.

I am strong.

I positively overcome obstacles that seem insurmountable.

I stand erect with posture that exudes confidence and self-belief.

I positively stand out in a crowd and attract other successful people to myself.

I carry myself with poise and self-assuredness.

CHAPTER 9
CONTACTING & INVITING

I am great at contacting and inviting my guests to view my opportunity.

I am a great listener. My ears are keen and in tune to potential prospects for my business.

I am relaxed and at ease when I talk to people such that they want to get to know me better and respect what I have to offer.

Everyone I prospect for my business becomes my business partner or customer.

I am able to discern which inviting technique and venue is best for my prospects.

My confidence and positive mental attitude supercedes any fear of rejection, fear of people, fear of talking to strangers and fear of the telephone.

I am bold and courageous and love people enough to share with them how this business can help them accomplish their dreams and goals.

I am no longer looking for the right person, I am the right person; therefore I attract the right people to my life and business.

I am a winner and I attract winners who are teachable, trainable and coachable.

I attract sharp ambitious people who are look ing for an opportunity to diversify their income portfolio.

Everyday, my path crosses with those who are influential, self-motivated, and have the ability to know, recognize and respond to opportunities.

I am so focused on my definiteness of purpose and goals that I share my business with everyone without reservation.

Everyday, my skill level increases in the area of contacting and inviting.

I master contacting and inviting and I am great at duplicating this throughout my group.

Sharp ambitious networkers are calling me on a daily basis wanting me to sponsor them into my business.

People, situations, and circumstances are arranged for me to meet, greet, and qualify the right people for my business.

I habitually attract and sponsor successful people who have an insatiable appetite to win and a tremendous work ethic.

CHAPTER 10
CREATING & MAINTAINING MOMENTUM

I am so happy and grateful to have one of the fastest growing teams and organizations in the company and industry.

My teammates and I are great at creating a sense of urgency for building at a rapid pace.

My organization has a culture of staying focused and prioritizing tasks according to income potential and team stability.

People on my team and in my organization have an insatiable appetite to win big and fast.

My team and I are great at mapping out the most effective and time efficient plan for our goals and desired promotions.

I am so excited and it feels so good to experience explosive exponential growth at such a rapid pace on our team.

My team grows exponentially every single month.

I love experiencing _____ % new growth in volume and new team members every single month.

The income of distributors in my organization is at an all time high such that there is a significant increase on a monthly basis.

People in my organization understand and master the principle of duplication such that we are experiencing a financial and team growth tsunami.

It feels so good to have the combination of such a healthy and sturdy business structure as well as team volume on a monthly basis.

My team's work ethic and results are huge reasons why our company progresses and hits critical mass and momentum.

My team members and I have a do-it-now mentality and all we do is win no matter what!

My team members and I are massive builders and promoters.

My team and I attend all events and are in tune to exposure opportunities at all times.

My team and I understand and commit to doing today what others won't so we can live tomorrow like others can't.

We are great at knowing our numbers so we can accurately predict and grow our numbers.

My team is clear about what it takes to hit their goals and build healthy structures which scientifically yield them the pin promotion they desire at the time they desire it.

Everyone on my team understands their plan of action to progress to their goals and commit to follow that course of action until they are successful.

CHAPTER 11
DECISION MAKING

I am great at making wise and timely decisions.

I attract and review all necessary information prior to making an informed decision.

I make intelligent choices.

I am considerate of others who are impacted by my choices and decisions.

I am great at quickly reviewing information and making quick and accurate decisions.

I am aware of my intuition and use discernment in my decision making when necessary.

I seek and obtain wise counsel prior to making critical decisions and when necessary.

I feel secure and wise when I obtain sufficient counsel regarding my decisions.

I am stable and fixed once I make a decision unless I realize the decision needs to be corrected or replaced.

I surround myself with wise decision makers and learn vicariously from others when given the opportunity.

I remain calm and relaxed as I make decisions.

I make sound judgments by finding feasible alternatives and choosing the one with the most potential for success.

I carefully weigh my options and rate them in order to choose the most favorable one that would yield the best result.

I harness my emotions to shape and strengthen my beliefs so that I reorganize my priorities and revise my goals when making decisions.

CHAPTER 12
DIAMOND STATUS

I, (your name)_____, am so happy and grateful now that I am a Diamond Consultant in (your company name) on or before (Date), enjoying the #1 lifestyle in the world.

I am no longer looking for the right people to come into my business because I am the right person.

I attract quality, serious, hungry, influential leaders to my business who possess a tremendous work ethic and discipline to complete and master tasks for them to succeed.

My business partners and leaders are teachable, trainable, coachable, and self-motivated.

My business partners and leaders have a will to work and win as well as a burning desire to succeed in this business.

Leaders on my team are quick learners, master duplicators and master promoters.

I have, I display and I use an abundance of wisdom and discernment for my desired goal this month and operate with extreme precision with getting my team members to their goals.

I know who to work with and properly prioritize my time and efforts.

As I identify and help others to hit their goals, I achieve my goals seemingly effortlessly.

My business partners and I have tremendous favor with everyone with whom we prospect for our business.

My leaders and I are on one accord and in agreement regarding their game plans and they execute their plans with precision and victory.

This month I personally sponsor at least _____ people and earn in excess of $ _____ with a monthly volume of _____ .

I look like a diamond! I think like a diamond! I make diamond-like decisions and I achieve diamond-like results because I am already a diamond!

Everyone my team members and I meet and prospect for this business gets started with the top packages upon hearing the plan.

People, events, resources and connections are divinely ordered and orchestrated such that I achieve diamond status this month with ease.

I qualify early and go back and help others complete their goals.

It feels so good to help so many people rank advance this month; consequently I rank advance to the Diamond pin level in _____ (company name) on or before _____ (date).

My team and I attract other successful people and ambitious networkers who are coachable with a large sphere of influence and an insa-

tiable appetite and work ethic to win in
_____(company name).

CHAPTER 13
DUPLICATING MASTERFULLY

It feels so good to be a master duplicator.

I am teachable, trainable and coachable; therefore I attract others who are the same way.

I am great at teaching those in my organization and teaching them how to effectively teach others in their organization.

I am great at evaluating and only participating in practices that are easily duplicatable.

I only adopt and institute philosophies and business practices that are in alignment with my goals, my team's goals and the company's goals.

I am great at attracting leaders who grasp concepts fairly easily and duplicate them well throughout their sphere of influence.

I am great at transferring my credibility to local leaders from other markets within my organization.

I am great at learning and teaching the skill sets necessary for a successful distributorship

My leaders and I exemplify the activity and work ethic we desire others to imitate in our group.

My team has and follows a systematic way of educating everyone we bring into the business.

My team is great at understanding and duplicating the skill sets that yield the most rewarding profits and results.

My team and I are great at leveraging our expertise and experiences as well as the experience and expertise of other top earners and industry leaders.

My team and I are committed to understanding and duplicating the system throughout our organization.

My team and I are great at instructing others as it relates to following the system and we lead by example.

My team and I are dedicated to attending events, showing the plan, and using the proper tools for team building and sustaining growth.

I am so happy and grateful now that my team and I duplicate the most profitable practices that yield the most positive and profitable results in our business.

My team and I attract self-motivated distributors who are committed to following and staying plugged into the system.

My team and I are great at creating leverage throughout our organization allowing us to do more with less effort, time and resources.

My team and I are great at sharing the product/service and opportunity in an effective manner.

My team and I are committed to keeping this business simple and we resist the urge to complicate it.

My core distributors, team members and I are committed to using the products/services that we promote.

Through the use of approved tools and technology, we duplicate success throughout our organization in record timing.

We attract quality business builders who are committed and skilled at duplicating successfully throughout the entire organization.

CHAPTER 14
FOLLOWING UP SUCCESSFULLY

I love following up with my prospects.

Follow ups are so fun to do especially since they yield extremely lucrative dividends.

I am great at following up with my prospects at the agreed upon time established during our previous interaction.

I make following up with my potential business partner or customer a top priority.

I easily establish rapport with my prospects during the onset of our meeting as well as during our follow up interactions.

I am keen and in tune to the needs of my prospects and refer back to them during the time of our follow up.

I have created a sense of urgency as it relates to following up my with prospects because the fortune is in the follow up.

I am so happy and grateful that everyone I follow up with either becomes a customer or a business partner.

I am committed to following up with my prospects within the first 48 hours or at the previously agreed upon time.

I am great at collecting the decision from my prospects and refraining from internalizing their responses.

I ask the appropriate questions in the most conducive manner during my follow up which ends up being in my favor.

I persist until I collect a decision from my prospect.

Following up with my prospect reveals that I am reliable and serious about my business.

I am great at keeping my word with my prospects regarding what I have promised to do.

I understand that following up and following through is critical to my success.

I am great at keeping my prospects informed about our company's growth and success as well as any new products or services.

I love asking for the sale, support, or referrals at the conclusion of the follow-up.

At the end of my interaction or appointment, I easily establish the next point of contact with my potential business partner/customer.

I exude confidence, poise, and a peaceful demeanor throughout my interaction with my potential business partner/customer.

CHAPTER 15
GOAL ATTAINMENT

I establish and maintain clear, specific, vivid, and attainable goals.

All of my goals are measurable with a congruent plan of action and a desired date of completion.

I daily engage in activity conducive to me attaining my goals.

I properly manage my self-talk or internal dialog and make the necessary adjustments in my thinking to support my dreams and goals.

I have 30-day activity plans clearly defining the activity in which I am committed to execute in order to attain my goals within the desired time frames.

I regularly review my goals and vividly picture my successful achievement of them.

It feels so good to achieve the goals I've established on or before the projected date of attainment.

My calendar reflects the activity necessary for successful achievement of my goals and allows me to accurately monitor my progression.

I am willingly accountable to those who support my goals and those who are aware of the established activities to which I have committed myself.

I successfully execute my plan with precision

and victory and reap the benefits thereof.

I properly reward myself upon completion of my goals.

CHAPTER 16
I AM

I AM POWERFUL!

I AM SUCCESSFUL!

I AM VICTORIOUS!

I AM AMAZING!

I AM INCREDIBLE!

I AM PROFITABLE!

I AM INSPIRATIONAL!

I AM TALENTED!

I AM GIFTED!

I AM ANOINTED!

I AM COMMITTED!

I AM WINNING!

I AM KINGLY!

I AM ROYALTY!

I AM EXCITED!

I AM PROMOTED!

I AM WEALTHY!

I AM LOVED!

I AM LOVELY!

I AM ATTRACTIVE!

I AM HEALTHY!

I AM SIGNIFICANT!

CHAPTER 17
LEADERSHIP

It feels so good to be a great leader.

I continuously commit to developing the leader within me and the leaders around me.

I have tremendous influence and charisma.

Everyone I lead respects my position and trusts me to help them get their desired results.

I am great at casting vision for myself and my team.

I am great at communicating the vision and keeping it before my teammates such that they adopt the vision as if it were contrived by them.

Those who I lead, love to buy in to what I suggest and advise.

I am great at getting people in my organization to do things I believe they should do while making them feel as though it is their idea.

I have excellent character as well as talent as a leader.

I have impeccable integrity and my word is my bond.

I am great at showing others in my organization how much I care about them and consequently they embrace and care about what I know and desire for them to understand and learn.

I am a great duplicator and a master promoter.

I am great at creating or mastering systems and duplicating this throughout my team.

I am great at identifying persons with whom I should invest my time, talents, and attention.

I have excellent people skills and I am a great communicator.

I only ask my teammates to do things that I am willing to do.

I am great at duplicating myself into others and finding capable successors.

I am committed to leading by example.

As a leader, I always rise to the occasion of my team and the "big-team" by meeting the need when I see one.

I love making more deposits than withdrawals as it relates to my family, team and company.

My choices and lifestyle positively encourage others within my organization and industry to do what is necessary to experience profitability at it's finest.

I am highly respected as a genuine and transparent leader throughout this company and industry.

I am great at showing compassion and when necessary "tough-love" to those I lead.

CHAPTER 18
LIST BUILDING

I am great at building a list of contacts to prospect for my business.

I have total recall as it relates to people with whom I have associated with in the past.

I have favor with people who I've done business with and I love adding them to my list.

I build a huge list of customers as well as potential business partners.

I am great at categorizing my list according to my prospects' qualities.

I daily meet new people to add to my list and refuel my pipeline.

I am great at discerning whether someone is a suspect or a qualified prospect.

I do not prejudge my prospects.

I release my mind from having to figure out if the prospect will actually be interested prior to my exposure.

I am great at qualifying my prospects.

I free myself from the pressure of knowing the outcome of my prospect's decision to engage my opportunity.

My list is filled with people who are influential,

self-motivated, coachable and financially able to start with the top start-up options.

I love including people on my list who I admire.

My list is full of people who have been extremely successful in their past ventures or activities.

I have a very impressive local list and distant list.

My list is comprised of people who have an insatiable appetite to win and succeed.

I am great at adding to my list people who have a large sphere of influence and lead me to others who love to win.

I have total recall of people who I've done business with and love adding them to my list because I have favor with them.

People love giving me referrals and leading me to others who are looking for what I have to offer.

CHAPTER 19
MASSIVE ACTION

I am great at beginning with the end in mind.

I remain focused on my desired outcome.

I am committed to succeed.

I am clear as to why I must succeed and commit to the process.

My core leaders and I are committed to taking massive action no matter what.

I am committed to visualizing my goal on a daily basis.

I reward myself after completing important tasks.

I am great at dividing the main goal into bite-size achievable tasks.

My energy and enthusiasm grows daily, motivating me to do more than I could have imagined I could do.

I have and attract the best support group, resources, technology, partners, and team members to help me increase my results in a more efficient manner.

I am great at working smart and not just working hard.

My team and I constantly attract others who de

cisively align their actions with their goals and desires.

I surround myself with others who are engaging in massive action.

I always listen and look at audio and visual material that motivate me to action.

It feels so great to achieve my goals in record time.

I am great at helping others on my team achieve the success they desire on or before their expected time periods.

It feels so good to be on this fast track and help others get on the fast track in this business.

I am great at casting vision to those on my team and clearly communicating the game plan.

My team and I proficiently execute the game plan prior to the established time lines.

I always go the extra mile and exceed the normal requirements or qualifications.

My team and I establish a habit of always performing above what is expected.

I harmoniously function in concert with the game plan for my desired results.

I excel at all I set my hands to do.

I am great at keeping myself motivated to take massive action and consequently, I achieve massive results.

I unreservedly take bold actions toward my goals.

I have a burning desire to achieve my goals; therefore I always take the required action.

I am so action-oriented that I conteract fear with direct action.

My consistent action creates undisputed momentum that propels others into massive action.

CHAPTER 20
MASTERING 3-WAYS
& EDIFICATION

I totally enjoy doing 3-way calls.

3-way calls are so fun to do!

I am extremely effective at facilitating 3-way calls between my expert and my prospect.

I am great at positively edifying my expert to my prospect prior to the 3-way appointment.

I am great at pre-establishing an appointment with my expert and showing respect for his/her time.

I am great at establishing how credible and successful my expert is to my prospect such that my prospect feels it is an honor to have the opportunity to talk with someone of his/her caliber.

I value the 3-way experience enough to attentively listen and take notes as my expert is talking to my prospect.

After my expert takes over the call, I am great at muting out my phone and quietly listening with the intent to learn the art of effectively doing a 3-way call.

I improve my 3-way skills every time I hear my senior partners conduct one.

When I am the expert in the 3-way call experience, I am great at establishing rapport with the prospect.

I am great at complimenting prospects and finding ways to relate to them.

I always remember to find out what information the prospect was exposed to and what they liked best about what they heard, saw, or experienced.

I am great at inviting prospects to make a buying decision or scheduling them for the next exposure opportunity.

I am an excellent story-teller and tell the story that is most conducive and relatable to the prospect.

As the expert, I am great at asking appropriate questions to get the prospects to influence themselves to make a commitment and feel good about it.

As the expert, I am great at validating the information the prospect heard during their exposure opportunity.

I love the 3-way call experience because it makes my building experience much simpler and rewarding.

I am alert and aware of techniques and strategies my expert uses to engage and commit my prospect.

My expert and I are so congruent that we harmoniously work well with one another, creating a pleasant and successful experience for all parties involved.

With ease, my expert retrieves pertinent information to sufficiently enroll our new business partner.

My confidence level tremendously increases in my ability to conduct successful 3-way calls every time I participate.

I am effective at teaching others in my organization how to master conducting and facilitating an effective 3-way call experience.

CHAPTER 21
MILLIONAIRE STATUS

I AM A MILLIONAIRE.

It feels so good to be a millionaire.

I walk like a millionaire.

I talk like a millionaire.

I live and give like a millionaire.

Everything I touch prospers and multiplies.

All of my investments yield me the greatest returns.

I wisely invest my time, talents, and treasures in the most profitable people, opportunities, deals, events, ministries, charities, and environments.

I love inspiring and developing others into millionaire status.

I am a great millionaire coach and I am committed to showing others how to create and sustain wealth.

I am a student of wealth and I am great at learning and applying wealth principles.

I am grateful to be a millionaire and possess great humility regardless of my status.

I understand the purpose for my millionaire status and properly use my influence and position as a millionaire to help uplift and inspire others.

I am an excellent giver and receiver.

I am so happy and grateful to be a millionaire and I remain humble.

I have a millionaire mindset!

CHAPTER 22
OVERCOMING FEAR OF FAILURE

I trust myself to make the right decisions.

I accurately calculate rewards, risks of opportunities, assignments, interactions and relationships.

I am totally at peace with decisions as it relates to my business and leadership.

I properly size up opportunities, tasks, and potential assignments.

I embrace "high-risk/high-reward" opportunities on a daily basis.

I understand and accept that high-risk opportunities yield me the greatest opportunities for promotion, reward and growth.

I am committed to overcoming any emotion that has the potential to hinder me.

I am committed to make my mark in this world and fulfill my purpose.

I mentally devour any giant or force attempting to abate or hinder my success.

My success is inevitable and I am committed to staying the course to see it through to completion.

I research all the potential outcomes (both good

and bad), increasing my ability to genuinely un derstand the risk of failure and the benefits of success.

I understand that the long-term benefits of my success far outweigh the short-term discom- forts.

I successfully take action upon the onset of any feelings of fear, thus increasing my chances to win and succeed.

I intelligently manage any perceived risks.

I am totally equipped to successfully deal with any situation that arises; therefore, I choose to invest my mental energy in going forward rather than focusing on back-up plans.

I am successful; I am a winner, and I am victori- ous in every situation.

All things work together for my good no matter how they initially appear or feel.

I am good at finding ways to grow from any un- successful attempts at my goals and making them eventually yield me a positive return.

I view failure as an opportunity to begin again; but this time more intelligently.

My eyes, ears, and heart are in tune to the equiv- alent seed of opportunity that accompanies any failure.

I embrace the idea that any perceived setback

is only a set up for a more rewarding comeback.

I successfully take on assignments and opportunities that stretch me.

I am a pioneer that embraces change and the process of upward mobility.

I understand that to walk on the water of success I must get out of the boat of my comfort zone and out of my own way.

I engage in activities that place a demand on my potential.

I do whatever it takes to release the talents and abilities that have been lying dormant in me.

I confidently take advantage of opportunities to use my gifts and fulfill my destiny.

This is my year to go beyond barriers of the past and release my potential by heading into uncharted territories.

There are unlimited possibilities on the inside of me and I am currently expanding my capacity to believe that I can do things I have never done before and succeed.

CHAPTER 23
OVERCOMING FEAR OF SUCCESS

I evict from my mind all disempowering thoughts and negative beliefs surrounding success and successful people.

I am good at replacing opposing thoughts regarding success with positive thoughts that embrace and support my acquisition and maintenance of success.

I deserve to be successful and embrace all the positives that can result from my success.

I have pleasant thoughts and experiences regarding success.

Success is my friend and I attract and embrace the idea and achievement of success.

I believe that successful people are good people who engage in gracious and kind acts that positively impact the lives of others.

I believe that successful people are "difference makers" and are fully loved and accepted by their creator, themselves, and others.

There is a need in our world for more successful people and I am great at supplying the demand by committing to be one of them.

It feels so good to be successful.

I am worthy of success.

I was created and engineered to succeed and make a positive mark in this earth.

I have a right to succeed, live an abundant life, and pursue happiness.

I possess everything I need, including the skill sets, abilities, wisdom, favor, people, funds, resources and connections to succeed.

Everyday my confidence level is increasing and I daily convince myself that I have what it takes to succeed.

I believe in myself and I have faith in myself to the point that success is my only option.

I possess a clear and positive vision for my life and my gifts make room for me to succeed.

I constantly reinforce the belief that I deserve to succeed and others need my example of success to encourage them to persevere.

My thoughts, beliefs, actions and results are in proper harmony and alignment with my achievement of meaningful success.

What other people think of me is none of my concern; therefore I release myself from the thoughts others have about my success.

I attract people to me who applaud my achievement and success and I have great relationships with other successful people who love to associate with me.

I view change and "moving forward experiences" as positive and necessary encounters that yield positively desired and meaningful results.

I inspire others to become successful.

I no longer worry about the future for it has the power to take care of itself, but I totally embrace the gift of today and commit to making the absolute most of it, moving forward and achieving significance.

I only attract positive people and experiences that support my attainment and maintenance of success.

I embody greatness and magnify the thoughts and actions that draw out of me that which has been within me all along.

Today, I reclaim my power to succeed and it feels victoriously awesome!

CHAPTER 24
OVERCOMING FRUSTRATION

I choose to be at peace and possess a pleasant disposition.

Because I have so much for which I am grateful, I willingly shift my focus from what initially did not happen the way I desired it to happen, to what is the next best course of action to gain my desired results.

I am aware of and choose to focus on techniques and strategies best suited to bring about my desired outcome.

I attract knowledgeable and more experienced people who are willing and available to invest their time, treasure, and wisdom to advise and enlighten me regarding perceived changes necessary in my planning to bring about my desired results.

I am "solution-oriented" and I attract the right solutions to my challenges.

I attract the best answers to my perceived obstacles.

When I don't get immediate results, I see an equal or greater seed of opportunity.

I take full responsibility for where I am and I choose to become better, stronger and wiser.

I take regular deep breaths and engage in the necessary physical activities that help reduce frustration and positively change my mood.

I have clear and resonate thoughts that support the changes I desire to see.

I change my environment when necessary and I give myself permission to release any guilt, condemnation, blame, or any other self-destructive or demeaning emotions.

I see myself succeeding and learning from all challenges.

I understand that any perceived setbacks are only set ups for positive comebacks.

I avoid rehearsing negative issues and refuse to participate in self-defeating internal dialog.

I choose to engage in activities and environments that help me feel better and good about myself.

I am not my behavior or my pin level.

My net worth is not attached to my self-worth.

I establish and commit to solve challenges by adopting and following an easy sequence of new orders.

I take full responsibility for where I am and I shift my focus from my current situation to where I desire to be.

This situation that I am currently experiencing is only temporary.

This challenge did not come to stay but it came to pass.

I am no longer a prisoner of my feelings.

It feels so good to be an overcomer and possess the victory in this situation.

I FEEL GREAT!

CHAPTER 25
OVERCOMING
PROCRASTINATION

I have a "prompt-to-do-it" attitude.

I execute tasks in a timely manner.

I accurately reduce my projects and goals into smaller tasks.

I possess the ability to get tasks done on or before time.

I am energized and motivated to fulfill my assignment and complete my goals.

I am good at rewarding myself throughout the completion of my goals and as I complete parts of my assignment.

I am committed to completing what I start and seeing every plan through to completion.

It feels so good to get started on tasks and not wait for perfect conditions.

I identify and successfully eliminate barriers and potential hindrances to my starting and completing tasks.

I am free of distractions to my starting and completing tasks.

It feels so good to finish what I start in a timely manner.

I work in intervals and I establish the proper priorities.

I am great at creating the conditions in my mind, emotions, environment and life that I need to succeed.

CHAPTER 26
PEOPLE MAGNET

I am a people magnet.

I chose to become the person I want to attract.

I have a pleasant personality and disposition.

Winners love being in my presence.

I possess the skill sets that attract successful people to me.

People who love what I have to offer positively gravitate towards me.

Wisdom easily flows from me to others who respect what I have to say.

I am attractive and appealing to others.

I look successful and carry myself with dignity and self-respect.

I am highly respected and well sought after for my wisdom and guidance, especially in this industry.

I attract the best business associates in alignment with my desired outcomes.

I attract people who are business savvy with an insatiable appetite to win and succeed.

I am great at leading myself and others.

I enjoy associating with people and putting myself in environments where I thrive.

People who encounter me always leave my presence better than when we initially interacted.

People have great anticipation of future interactions with me because of my winning personality and how I make them feel.

CHAPTER 27
PEOPLE SKILLS

I am contagiously positive.

I have great people skills.

I am genuinely interested in other people.

I have a winning smile and I have a habit of smiling all of the time.

I easily win friends and influence people.

I am a dynamic listener.

I listen more than I talk.

My tonality and body language are congruent with what I desire to communicate verbally.

I have an approachable demeanor and disposition.

People feel at ease and comfortable while in my presence.

I am great at identifying and recognizing people for the positive things they do.

I am great at getting people to do what I suggest and desire while making them feel that it is their idea.

I am quick to admit my errors or misjudgments when I am wrong.

I am great at validating people's feelings and values.

People actually leave my presence more esteemed than when they entered it.

When I correct or give caring feedback to others, I do it with compassion and without arousing resentment or offense.

When I provide constructive feedback, I begin and end with praise and honest appreciation.

I often share my own mistakes before giving critical feedback to others.

I am great at asking questions instead of giving direct orders.

I am great at encouraging others and making sufficient deposits so that I earn the right to make withdrawals when necessary.

I am great at identifying people's temperament or personality types and quickly adapt my approach to increase my communication effectiveness with them.

I am great at remembering a person's name and I pronounce it correctly and often enough during communication so that rapport is easily established and maintained.

My demeanor easily repels drama and negative communication.

I am great at disarming conflict and mediating between team members when necessary.

I easily win the trust and respect of my peers and those I lead.

I am a great team player and I work extremely well with others.

I am great at esteeming others more highly than myself.

CHAPTER 28
PERSEVERENCE

I persist past my feelings or any desire to give-up, cave in or quit.

I am unstoppable!

I quickly see the opportunity to win even during challenging times.

What I see now is only temporary and no condition is permanent.

I am great at making the necessary corrections and adopting the changes and philosophy necessary for growth and desired results.

All things are working together in such a way that I win in spite of any opposition or how it currently looks.

I am great at breaking records during times of adversity.

I am like a palm tree in that I'm flexible, resilient and have "bounce-back" ability.

I positively bounce back better, stronger, and wiser from every challenge.

I optimally use resistance as a spring board for positive growth, promotion and expansion.

I am not moved by what I see, hear or feel, only by what I believe I deserve and what I was promised.

My work ethic is congruent with the goals I have set to obtain.

I maintain the proper perspective indicative of a winner, and persist past any perceived obstacles.

I am so resilient!

I AM VICTORIOUS!

CHAPTER 29
PIN ACHIEVEMENT

I am a _____ (desired pin name).

It feels so good to achieve the _____ pin level.

I am so amazed that I obtain more volume than what I need to achieve the _____ pin level.

It feels good to be recognized and respected as a _____ (pin name) in _____ (company name).

I exceed the income expected for someone at the _____ pin level.

It feels good to experience the wonderful combination of both pin and profitability.

I walk and talk like a _____ (pin name).

I make decisions like a _____ (pin name) and I experience the results achieved by _____ (pin name).

I am great at attracting everything I need to achieve my desired pin level.

I have an impressively positive structure in alignment with my desired pin level.

I am great at attracting quality leaders, resources, connections, and favorable events that help me yield the _____pin level on or before my expected date of _____.

I am very clear on the activity and mindset necessary to achieve the _____ pin level and I am great at helping others in my group promote to this level as well.

I have more than the amount of people suggested showing the plan, sharing the product/ services, attending events, and using the tools.

I attract and follow through on the knowledge of why and how to achieve the _____ pin level and exceed the guidelines and expectations.

Once I obtain the _____ pin level, I always re-qualify until I qualify at the next highest level consistent with my business structure and activity.

CHAPTER 30
PROMOTING EFFECTIVELY FOR EVENTS

I am a master promoter.

I love promoting for events.

I make sure people are excited about attending the next event.

I am a great example to those I lead in that I am always registered early, and I am always promoting for the next event.

I successfully work my business from event to event.

I am great at scheduling events for my group before and after the next major event.

I am great at getting my leaders fired up about promoting for events.

I effectively teach and recognize others within the group who are mastering the art of promotion.

I am effective at influencing my team to have pre-established goals and activities prior to the event.

I am great at creating a sense of urgency and value for attending events.

I understand that I must do more than an

nounce the event; therefore I effectively promote for the event with intensity.

I am great at identifying and restating the hot buttons of those I lead and properly showing them how attending events is an important step in getting them to their desired goal.

I am so happy and grateful that those on my team who commit to attend an event actually show up with a burning desire to receive a breakthrough and reinforce their commitment.

I am excellent at creating anticipation for attending the event by sharing how this is a once in a lifetime opportunity and a "don't-miss" event.

My leaders and I always attend all events we qualify to attend.

I am great at adjusting my language to the temperament of the person with whom I am promoting.

I am extremely proficient at training others how to promote effectively for events.

I am great at using words that move people to action.

It feels so good to be a master promoter like Don King.

It feels so good to have _____ (amount) people at the next event.

I am great at scientifically tracking my numbers and exponentially growing the number of people who attend events from my organization.

My team and I are great at pre-qualifying prospects who should attend events so that they positively experience our culture, buy into the company's vision, and expand their capacity to believe that our vehicle can help them accomplish their goals.

CHAPTER 31
PUBLIC SPEAKING/
COMMUNICATING

I love my audience and my audience loves me.

What I have to say is so empowering and substantive that my audience literally hangs onto my words.

I say the right things in the right way to everyone with whom I speak.

I treat my presentations and trainings as if I'm merely having a highly valued conversation.

I am great at discerning what my audience needs to hear.

I am great at story-telling, using metaphors and purposeful humor when necessary to effectively communicate.

I am great at painting pictures with my words thus effectively communicating what I want my audience to understand.

My audience is attentive and desire to receive what I communicate.

I view my audience as friendly listeners who need and want to hear what I have to share.

I am great at sharing my ideas and concepts with others.

My voice and tonality are always pleasant and appropriate to those listening to me.

This conversation I am having with my audience has nothing to do with me and everything to do with them and our cause.

I am free of distractions, disempowering thoughts and negative nuances or feelings while I am speaking.

My words bring enlightenment to those who are listening.

People always leave my presence empowered and better equipped to win.

My thoughts flow freely when I share with others.

People value what I have to say and they respect my wisdom.

Wisdom emanates from my lips when I talk.

I only speak when I have something relevant to share and I speak for the right reasons.

I know when to talk and when to listen.

I am great at using active listening techniques with those with whom I am speaking.

I demonstrate that I am always present in the moment and I value what others have to say.

CHAPTER 32
RETENTION

I have one of the fastest growing organizations in my company and in the industry.

People who join my organization love being in my organization.

My team has tremendous team spirit.

People on my team feel welcomed and valued as members of the team.

I am great at validating those who are on my team.

I use tremendous discernment in my coaching and interacting with teammates.

People on my team and in my company feel empowered and possess a positive sense of belonging.

My leaders and I are great at coaching and assisting people on the team to get the best results and establish remarkable 30-day stories.

People in my organization are committed to personal growth and they persevere past insurmountable obstacles.

People on my team get off to a fast start and are effective at helping others get off to a great start.

People in my organization are profitable and great at managing their own and other's expectations.

I have impressive statistics as it relates to those actively working the business in my organization.

Every month, my retention percentages are increasing.

Even the incubators in my organization are committed to their monthly service or product order.

My leaders and I are great at leading at the top of our organization and working at the bottom, creating and duplicating momentum.

CHAPTER 33
SELF-DISCIPLINE

I willingly do what is right especially when no one else is looking.

I willingly adopt the thoughts, behaviors, actions and habits in alignment with my established goals.

I am in control of my thoughts.

I persevere in action tasks relevant to my goals whether I feel like it or not.

I am so focused on my desired outcome that I am not moved by what I see, hear, or feel.

I am so convinced that the long-term benefits of accomplishing my goals far outweigh any short-term discomforts.

I am unstoppable!

I am steadfast, unmovable and always abounding in activities in alignment with my desired outcome.

I persevere and persist past any discomfort that is a perceived hindrance to me achieving my goal.

I exercise supportive power and control over my actions and behavior.

I command my will to align with my desired outcomes.

I have incredible self-control.

I am dedicated to staying on track.

I easily resist any desires that would jeopardize me achieving my desired results.

I only crave things that would propel me further in obtaining my goals.

I only accept urges that support my desired outcome.

I resolve that it is always too soon to quit.

My "will-power" is like a muscle, the more I exercise it, the stronger it becomes.

CHAPTER 34
SUCCESSFUL

I am extremely successful in all that I do.

I attract success everywhere I go.

I love success and success loves me.

I love being successful.

The door of success is open wide to me because I deserve to be successful.

I also deserve to enjoy all that success embodies.

I am well-equipped to obtain and sustain success.

I am totally comfortable with being successful.

I embrace success as it is a normal outcome for me.

I have successful relationships and business transactions.

I engage in successful activities which bring about the best results and desired outcomes.

I am clear about what I want out of life and I am committed to successfully carrying out my life's mission.

I am great at making room for success in my life.

CHAPTER 35
TEAMWORK/TEAM DEVELOPMENT

My team and I work well together.

We have great team spirit and a healthy respect for one another.

Our team morale is 100% positive all of the time.

We have one of the most admired teams in the company and industry.

Our team leaders are unified and easily flow in concert with one another.

When working with one another and other teams, we synergize our efforts for the good of the company.

We represent the "one team one dream" motto.

My team represents _____ % of the company's distributors and contributes _____% of the company's sales volume.

My team has market share in the following market(s): _____.

My teammates and I attract other sharp and ambitious team players to our team and understand how to flow as a cohesive unit.

My team has a spirit of excellence in all that we do.

My team and I understand that we represent our families and the company even during our leisure time and our behavior reflects this understanding.

My team and I enjoy being the supporting cast for one another and cheering for the success of those on and off our team.

My team values the "big team" over just our team and only engages in behavior that exudes this philosophy.

My team philosophy is in alignment with the company's core philosophies.

CHAPTER 36
TIME & LIFE MANAGEMENT

I am great at managing my time and managing my life.

I establish the appropriate guidelines and boundaries to protect my time.

I always get the best return on the time I invest into people, projects, events, and activities.

I prioritize my time according to purpose and income potential.

I respect the power of leverage and attract people, systems, situations, events, tools and resources to help me maximize my time.

I respect the time I've been allotted to carry out specific tasks and work accordingly.

I value my time as well as other people's time.

Time is my friend and we respect one another.

I get more accomplished during shorter time periods.

I effectively manage my time.

I effectively plan my time and time my plan in such a way that I achieve record results.

I properly organize my schedule to achieve the most effective results.

I daily make an "achievement list" comprised of

things I plan to achieve for today and enjoy checking them off as they are accomplished.

I wisely use my time to prepare and organize.

I always work on high priority tasks first.

I understand that my time is just as valuable as money; therefore I use it wisely.

I greatly protect my time from being misused by anyone, even myself.

I control what I do with my time.

Properly using my time is an investment which yields tremendous dividends.

I put my time to the best possible use.

I plan my work and effectively work my plan within the allotted time frames.

I always finish my desired tasks on or before the time they are due.

I am timely for all my appointments, events, conference calls, and briefings.

I am great at discerning how much time to allot for various tasks and activities.

CHAPTER 37
WORK ETHIC

I have a tremendous work ethic.

My work ethic is extremely admired by others.

I have a mind to work and a discipline to finish what I start.

My positive perspective regarding the tasks I need to complete increases my productivity.

I enjoy sharpening and improving my skills.

I do today what others won't so I can live tomorrow like others aspire to live.

I understand that the long-term benefits and promotions far outweigh the short-term discomforts of my work.

I take pride in the work I do such that I give it 100% when I am engaged with it.

I love to work smart and systematize my efforts.

I reward myself along the way for improvements and progression made toward my desired goals.

I attach the most motivating "fear of loss" or "desire for gain" to my goal and allow it to inspire me to actively work toward my goal until it is realized.

It feels so good to excel at all that I do.

I am great at only receiving and implementing coaching from "one-voice" or those who are already successful and have a vested interest in my success.

I approach my business and goals with a bulldog's tenacity.

I masterfully overcome any obstacle to completing my tasks and visibly see it as an opportunity that pays me huge dividends once I conquer it.

I love engaging in work that is both fulfilling and lucrative.

My attitude exudes that I am happy with what I am doing so much that it's challenging to distinguish between whether I am working or playing.

CHAPTER 38
SAY IT UNTIL YOU SEIZE IT
SELF-CONTRACT

I, _____, hereby agree and commit to verbalize, visualize, and emotionalize my success on a daily basis until it manifests. I am committed to saying it until I seize it because I believe it's my time to win.

Affirmations of Focus: **Victory Date**

1. _____   _____

2. _____   _____

3. _____   _____

4. _____   _____

5. _____   _____

Personal Affirmation

I am so happy and grateful now that _____

_____

_____

_____(insert your goal or desire).

Other Books & Recordings By Author:

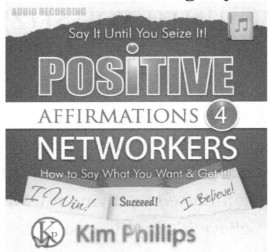

AUDIO SERIES: POSITIVE AFFIRMATIONS 4 NETWORKERS

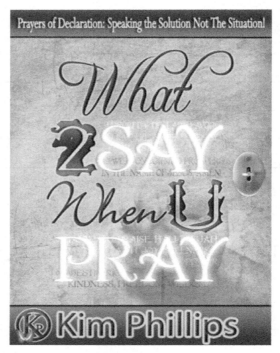

Book: What 2 Say When U Pray

ABOUT THE AUTHOR

Kim Phillips is an inspirational speaker, life strategist, success mentor and transformational leader who is often referred to by her colleagues and peers as "Harriet Tubman Junior" because of her commitment to help others gain their financial, spiritual, emotional, mental, and interpersonal freedom. Agreeing with Jim Rohn's philosophy that "formal education will make you a living while self-education will make you a fortune", she has definitely demonstrated a value for both educational journeys. Kim is quickly becoming known as an affirmation specialist and is affectionately called the "affirmation queen" by many in her industry mainly because she strategically rearranges words and wisdom with oratorical finesse. After reading her books, you may agree that affirmations and declarations seem to effortlessly emanate from her as she passionately instructs others how to use their words to design their desired situations.

Contact Information: Book us to speak to your group or contract us to design a personal affirmation for you or your team. **www.kimphillipstoday.com**

Made in the USA
Middletown, DE
16 February 2024

49585050R00076